Times, Times, and times again
My days turn into nights,
I have this little girl of mine
And must keep her from freights,

She is my darling I adore
With each smile and cry,
I love her dearly, yes I do
And will until I die,
As a mother new and true
Some things weren't so clear,
Of how I'd bond with this child
And how I'd feel so near,
She is the very breath I breathe
She is my pride and joy,
I give her all my essense be
All I can employ,
I thank God for her to be
Safely in my arms,
And as all mothers are to be
I'll keep her safe from harms,
To all mothers want to be
I just have this to say,
When your child is in your arms
Your nights will turn to day.

Joel David Phifer
August 6, 2023

The Spirit's Call

Juliana

A newborn baby gives and breathes life into every mother. Though days and nights blend together, the love is unparalled with all else known.

God did this by design. It is only when we know love as a parent, that we realize the Depth of Love he has towards us.

God Bless you and your family

J. David Phelps

August 6, 2023

The Spirit's Call

Joel David Kilgore

Joel David Kilgore
2023

Version 3: 2023

ISBN: 978-1-365-74643-7

Joel David Kilgore
P.O. Box 1271
Manassas, VA 20108

Dedication

To my loving daughters Gloria and Moriah. Their cherishing of the poems within this book have touched my heart.

To my loving mother which, in her lifetime, was delighted to read anything the spirit allowed me to write.

To God for trusting me with a gift that calls unto his spirit and binds poetry into and from lives.

Contents

Acknowledgements

I would like to thank my friend Roger Holmes for constantly asking me to compile these poems for publication. He constantly reminded me that many folks could appreciate these writings, which helped make this publication a reality.

Preface

At an early age of 16 years old I prayed in faith to Christ for the ability to write poetry. Not just any poetry, but a gift that would bind hearts back to God and explain God's mysteries. I never wanted to receive credit for any of the writings, but rather wanted to acknowledge that the gift was from God, and he only should receive any recognition for any poem received. God answered the prayer, and I began to write. When writing begins, I feel an inward draw to document the poem. It is as if the poem is being born and is alive, but also has always existed. The draw, or rather God's spirit's call "pulls" at my spirit, and I generally hear only the first few words as I begin to write. What follows is the rest of the poem, word-by-word, and line-by-line. I cannot change the writings nor forcibly try to write. For that reasoning, I do not feel that I am the true author for any of the poems within this book. God is the true author, and I am merely the vessel of delivery for these texts.

The poems within this book bear witness of God's greatness, are written for individuals, or to the general populace.

Introduction

If any of the readers of this small book can find a word of encouragement, then it is very worth all the effort in compiling and publishing. The gifts from God are not driven or owned by the recipients, but rather a charge to acknowledge and let the gifts manifest and minister in the spirit of the gift. God allowed me a gift of poetry, and I pray to always keep in mind and heart that the gift is not for my benefit, but for those of whom the spirit of God calls and touches.

This book is a compilation of the poems written to or for individuals, in prayer or praise to God, or just in general. The poems in this book were written for various occasions and a variety of subjects. Personally, I find it difficult to take any credit for the poems. I thank God for his spirit, I thank God for his presence, and I thank God for his gifts.

The Spirit's Call

A Little Grandchild

I have a little grandchild
With a smile as wide as sky,
I have a little grandchild
That always asks me why,

I'm asked at times for candy
I'm asked at times for gum,
I'm asked if I am hungry
I'm asked to play, have fun,

I seldom get to see him
But when I do I know,
That we will play together
As grand kin e'er do so,

I have a little grandchild
That sees me as a toy,
And as such I see him too
This cute little boy,

When e'er his parents calling
For him to please behave,
I'll run the interference
And will till I'm in grave,

I have a little grandchild
And as more I look, I see,
The beauty of this grandchild
I see in his eyes - - me.

A Little Pepper

If I had a little pepper
I'd make a jar of sauce,
I'd keep it in my cabinets
And not let it get lost,

I'd use it when I'm fishing
To make my bait tasty,
To catch a sharky critter
Within the depth of sea,

I'd fricassee this critter
And serve it on my boat,
With friends who've joined in feasting
The critters I would tote,

If I had a jar of hot sauce
To make the meal so fine,
I'd use it on the critters
That I've caught with my line,

If I had a little critter
That jumped into my plate,
I'd think of all the critters
That in my past I ate,

If I had a little pepper
And had a little time,
I'd make my own concoction
With flavors that are mine,

If I had to find a reason
To make my "ifs" come true,
I'd find myself relaxing
Upon an ocean blue,

In life my "Ifs" are journeys
With each its merit path,
Which give my 'ifs' a reason
To hold them while life lasts,

For every "ifs" a journey
And every "had's" a hope,
And dreams are spun from wishing
From what our heart evokes,

If I had a little pepper
With just a little time,
I'd add the hope of wishing
And dreams within my mind.

A Time of Life

A time of life -- a life in time
We live to know each other,
Our spirits tie with those we love
Father, mother, sister, brother,

From children grand to parents old
Our hearts are filled with love,
To keep them close and hold them dear
As designed -- from God above,

We seek to know the reason
For life's humble fragileness,
Not knowing for a season
Of why we have this bliss,

We live to know each other
To treat ourselves as one,
In good times and in bad times
From time that life begun,

To hold each other dearly
That love will ever grow,
Encompassing hereafter
These things we all should know,

Once the life is over
It really does not end,
Our spirit finds a freedom
In God's kingdom where we mend.

In Memory of
Grace Dorothy Demma
1919-2014

A Wish in Time

Hours are numbered
Days are named,
Weeks do end
And start again,

Months bring seasons
Of the year,
Nights bring stars
Which shine so clear,

Years bring wisdom
Spirit's truth,
We grow away
From our once youth,

All in all
These words be said,
The message in
What is read,

Is that this day
You find so special,
And from its truth
To never wrestle,

Be of cheer
And mirthful way,
Enjoying full
This your birthday!

Anna "Morgana" Nash

The trouble with all pirates
In my domestic view,
Is how they are all scattered
From danger not eschewed,

Without a union forming
They pay to no one dues,
Without a true direction
They gain from nothing new,

Their tattered boats and clothing
Leaves nothing to respect,
Their constant greed and loathing
Will leave our seas a wreck,

Their tyrant's way of plunder
Respects no mortal man,
The flags that they fly under
Is war with every land,

They need a true persuasion
That stands the test of time,
To give to every nation
Of pirate's pros and rhyme,

If I were but their leader
I'd make them understand,
That plunder has no reason
And better views of man,

I'd make them wash their tatters
And clean coral from crafts,
To fly a flag of stronghold
Clean ships from bow to aft,

I'd have them form a union
And pay the pennied dues,
And make a conference table
To think their plunders through,

If I were but a pirate
I'd take my ship ashore,
And lead them in the battles
That triumphs pirate's lore,

The trouble with all pirates
Is that they cannot see,
Is that their mass confusion
Can be answered - - just by me!

Anticipation's Season

Blinking bright and twinkling
The colors bold and true,
Festive eves of merriment
In nature's themes and hues,

We find ourselves in joyous tunes
Our mood is filled with glee,
We spend our gold on everything
Of what we hear, we see,

The season full of rush and wait
The days are short and few,
The time we spend with family
Not knowing what we do,

We wrap our gifts in bows and ties
We place them neath a tree,
We yearn our loved one's merriment
And for them mirth to be,

This night each year repeated
And yet each time we find,
Our eyes upon that season
Is only in our mind.

Awakening

Eastern stars are shining
Day has slipped away,
Ties that bind are finding
Night has come to stay,

Days of all surroundings
Find the tearful end,
All our faint hearts pounding
Seek to make amends,

Christ the king of glory
To the battle cry,
He will end the story
And we will never die,

All the grief around us
The bitter and the dry,
All the ties that bound us
Won't keep us from the sky,

Christ, his spirit calling
To claim of each his own,
Rises to his glory
And claims his rightful throne,

All the life around us
Lives within his care,
We're thankful that he found us
And of his spirit share,

Now within the kingdom
There reigns our Lord and King,
Al-le-lu we cry out
To him we ever sing,

In the glorious triumph
We lost the bitter woes,
And now to God we give all
Of praise and all that goes,

There within God's kingdom
Where is no earthly care,
But songs of praise hereafter
Forever fill the air,

Unto us he's calling
To know the bitter end,
Is not for us to live for
But reach to God as friend,

All life's bitter moments
Sorrow and the lies,
All the inner darkness
Can't keep us from on high,

If we know the secret
To life's eternity,
To know that Christ the savior
Rose to set us free,

When you hear him calling
Answer with your heart,
His grace is never falling
And from you he won't part,

Now you know the secret
Now you've seen the day,
Now you know the answer
Now you know to pray.

Joel.david.Kilgore@Gmail.Com

The Battle

Marching to a battle
Fighting with a foe,
Ever-restless days on end
Wrestling toe to toe,

Keeping all that matters
Deep within the soul,
Clearing way to victory
To our nation's goal,

Every day these warriors
Keep our foes at bay,
Protecting friendly borders
Thru relentless ways,

Knowing friends and loved ones
Are their protected goal,
Knowing brothers' battle
With enemies untold,

All our hearts are with them
We hold them up in prayer,
They fight for our freedoms
At times we're unaware,

The soldiers are our family
Our fathers, brothers, sons,
They teach us that no sacrifice
Is too great for victories won,

The battle ever weary
The wars are all the same,
Our soldiers never bending
To defeat nor to shame,

In moments of tense fighting
In times of deafening lull,
In throes of extreme brilliance
These warriors make their cull,

They'll not give into dismay
They'll not run from the field,
But rather quash the sundry
And gain the victory's yield.

Celebrate

The seasons and the reasons
Are not difficult to see,
We glamorize each moment
Of days of jubilee,

With Easter comes the rabbit
With eggs all strewn all around,
Forgetting Christ the savior
Who chose the cross for crown,

We choose a day of loving
With chocolates all around,
Forbidding it's for lovers
Of the joy they both have found,

We speak of our Thanksgiving
With suppers mirth and glee,
But rarely are we thankful
Of how this land came to be,

Of Christmas morn we gather
With presents under tree,
Forgetting Christ the savior
And how he set us free,

With all these tender moments
Of holidays we cast,
We tend to send the greetings
Of what will never last,

It's not the fluffy rabbit
Nor eggs upon the ground,
It's of the birth of Jesus
And joys that we have found,

It's not the cupid's arrow
Nor chocolate in the hand,
It's of the heart filled longing
In all woman and all man,

It's not the feasting table
That stuffs our bellies so,
But of a country able
To ride the seasons flow,

It's not the caroled Kringle
With man red clothed with beard,
But of the birth of savior
Who is both loved and feared,

We let the seasons pass us
And send our greetings vast,
While truth of time will cast us
As with forgotten past!

Christmas

The night is called Christmas
As we look to give,
Good gifts of friendship
To those whom we live,

We seek to be merry
And happy in heart,
But so rarely we think
Why did this all start?

It started in Israel
Some centuries ago,
In a Bethlehem stable
On a night that did glow,

The shepherds were watching
Their flocks late that night,
When an angel came to them
In clothes fair and bright,

The angel brought tidings
Of one who was born,
And laid in a manger
In clothes that were worn,

"The king of all heaven
is now sent to you,
Go honor and praise him
As this we now do,"

The shepherds did hasten
To see who was born,
In a Bethlehem stable
On that Christmas morn,

The shepherds found wise men
Who brought with them gold,
And many more gifts
For the babe they were told,

It happens at Christmas
The day which we see,
To give all men presents
With laughter and glee,

The children with laughter
The parents with smiles,
And under the trees
Are great Christmas piles,

We think of Kris Kringle
With little green elves,
And have long red stockings
Hanging from shelves,

We open our hearts
And empty our heads,
Of why this occasion
Is so widely spread,

The birth of the savior
God's present to men,
The greatest of gifts
- - Abolishes sin!

Christmas Theme

It happens every year you know
The Christmas shopping scene,
We give gifts of wondrous cheer
To show the love we mean,

With cheer we give we sing a song
With joy within the season,
Sometimes we may hardly know
The first gift and the reason,

If truth be told in days of old
The birth of Christ and star,
The wise men with the gifts of three
And how they traveled far,

We with our gifts may e'er forget
The birth immaculate,
The gift from God that started all
And of this cycle set,

As we give we should e'er be
Always within our means,
And honor him whom gave his Son
So, we could be redeemed.

Color Blind

My eyes do not see color
In nature's truest way,
For grass and hay look much the same
In lightness of the day,

My eyes do not see color
As normal as they be,
Though shapes and sizes I define
Hughes are hard to see,

I know Kentucky grass is green
With a tint of blue I'm told,
Of this beauty I confess
Mt eyes may not behold,

Some contrasts I cannot see
The beauty nor the shame,
I wonder how this world would be
If people appeared the same?

How would it be if every man
Instead of viewing skin,
Searched deep and far beyond the flesh
To that which lies within?

The Commitment

Lord, I took a wife today
I gave my oath of love,
I held her hand and kissed her lips
Our match fits like a glove,

I find I'm always flirting
And stealing kisses too,
Our desires are unswerving
As when we said, "I do,"

I see the smile that builds me
The joyous breath I breathe,
Is due to her that thrills me
And what in her I see,

The mornings' filed with laughter
The daytimes' filled with fun,
The evenings' filled with passion
As our journey has begun,

I see her eyes that twinkle
Which makes my heart run fast,
Her voice is as a sprinkle
Which makes my yearnings last,

I look for each tomorrow
When I lay down to sleep,
In her I have no sorrow
She has my heart to keep,

I always ask to realize
This gift you've given man,
This love of life that calls for
Each day to take her hand.

The Communicator

I went to talk and tell a tale
To be so understood,
I thought my theme and structure clear
And heard by all who would,

My meaning in my spoken voice
To every lending ear,
Seemed to me epiphany
And to all to be quite clear,

My flowing verse and rhyming sound
Was music to the soul,
The thoughts be heard of all around
Seemed to make one whole,

The evidence of what I said
Beamed from every face,
My thoughts invoked imagined
To every man and race,

When asked of listeners later
To recall words I said,
A shock of awe flew through me
My pride in speech quite fled,

The words that I imagined
That caught my listener's ear,
Weren't used in the same fashion
My meaning wasn't clear,

The dialog of people
Within each given land,
Has broad and confined meanings
And different to each man,

Of my understanding
I spoke and chose my text,
Not knowing words demanded
Known by whose standing next,

When if e'er I choose again
To speak a speech so bold,
I'll seek to know the meaning
Of words as local told.

The Dreamer's Dream

Last night I dreamt of dreaming
Of inner thoughts and things,
My greatest fear and love I lost
Of near and dearest things,

I dreamt oft times of flying
Yet never in a plane,
I dreamt once of my dying
And yet I live again,

I dreamt of resurrection
Yet have no memory there,
I dreamt of life's succession
Of things I dare not care,

I've dreamt of my surroundings
Of why I do not know,
I've dreamt of trumpets sounding
Of stories never told,

I've dreamt of true believing
In faith above all things,
Of spirits e'er ascending
With angelectic wings,

I've dreamt internal dreaming
Of times that I awoke,
Yet still in dreamer's dreaming
My inner fears evoke,

I've dreamt of life hereafter
Of why I should e'er dream,
Of solitary chapters
Of what dreams are to mean,

And yet in all my dreaming
The answer should be clear,
I dream my life's ambitions
And things I greatly fear,

A word to all the dreamers
To follow lessons learned,
Of what the soul is saying
In images it churns,

Let not your heart be troubled
To find out what it means,
To learn life's truest lessons
Within the dreamer's dream.

The Grandchild

As grandkids go
They are such fun,
They make us laugh
They love to run,

Their loving smiles
Their twinkling eyes,
With each day
A new surprise,

We hear them laugh
We feel them cry,
We love them so
We can't say "bye,"

They hold our hearts
We hold their hands,
They're precious in
Most every land,

Within their eyes
We see them play,
Within their voice
They light the day,

With every question
That they ask,
It gives to us
A humbled task,

With each moment
Of this child,
We find ourselves
So tender mild,

When e'er they're here
Or we are there,
Each moment spent
Is one that is shared.

The Higher Stand

Ever pressing, ever needing
Looking towards that great divide,
Make our reasons for the season
Be the workings of our stride,

If accepting - not rejecting
A challenge newer than before,
We will make choice of conscious
And make our way-full path secure,

If our interest be in gaining
If our motions be not jest,
If our intents be abstaining
We will win and be our best,

On to pastures ever greener
On to limits high and bold,
On to victory in our season
On to riches yet untold,

Keep in mind as we ponder
Goals defined in our grasp,
We will win if we don't wander
From what our heart has put to task.

How Long?

From time of birth till end of days
A question lingers on,
It asks of God in spirit truth
A course life follows on,

How long shall our hearts endure
The distance from the King?
With worship high and spirits share
The praises we do sing,

How long the stand that we take
To show the world the King?
Of all demands the world makes
And knows not the heaven's ring,

Of our distance from the King
How long do we wait?
To hear the triumph of the horn
To walk through heaven's gate?

How long the battle of the soul
The cries of faith therein?
How long endure the natural flesh
How long to battle sin?

How long to hear the King's command
"It's finished, all is done"?
How long to journey in this land
Till all the victories won?

How long the vision of our soul
Be clouds of fleshy veil?
How long till all our spirits know
That God will never fail?

How long will doubt fight our faith?
To try to steal the soul?
How long till ends this spirit race
Until the final goal?

Never ending question's
A never-ending path,
As souls will seek a reason
And of that reason ask,

How long to all fulfillment
Of prophecies of old?
How long till we are standing
In heaven's streets of gold?

Perhaps the best of questions
Is not of why how long,
But instead, our spirits question
Ourselves - - our faith— How Strong?

I Am

The reasons I am
And the reasons to be,
Are not convoluted
As they seem to be,

In all my journeys
In all my days,
In all my learning
In all my ways,

I see daily futures
I see morning tasks,
I see paper headlines
I see questions asked,

I hear all the banter
I hear spirit woes,
I hear morning rush hour
I hear as days go,

My place here amongst them
Is not just to be,
But watch them, weigh them
Then let them see me,

Let all with their vision
And all with their pride,
See what's inside me
As they see my stride,

I'll not look to heaven
For what I can do,
I'll not blame a failure
On spirits eschewed,

I'll not place a heartbreak
On a pedestal high,
I'll not place salvation
Higher than sky,

I choose to be different
I choose to be me,
I choose to let others
See me as free,

Free from the worries
Free from the games,
Free from the fetters
Free from false fame,

Now that you see
All reasons of me,
You'll know why I chose
In this life - - to be free.

I Know A Man

I know a man
That lived in Galilee
I see him in my daily prayers
And he lives inside of me

I know a man
That came from God's own throne
He took my sins to Calvary
And made them all his own

I know a man
That makes the blind to see
His life is filled with miracles
Which touch both you and me

I know a man
That reaches to my soul
He calls me to his harmony
To make my life be whole

I know a man
That left a dying tomb
He rose up from the dead
And healed from all his wounds

I know a man
That we'll crown the King of Kings
He's God in flesh manifest
Of his glory we all sing

I know a man
That lives within my heart
He teaches me what's right and wrong
And says He'll never part... I know a man
I know - - a man.

It Rings

It rings, it talks, it lights my way
It tells where I should be today,
It entertains and helps me sing
I answer it on friendly rings,

It lets me see the internet
It tells the weather -- dry or wet,
It tells me what my friends have said
By texts and blogs that I have read,

It keeps me current in the know
Of what friends do and where they go,
It is my journal through the day
And transmits all I have to say,

I walk and read it like none other
With eyes held tightly to this lover,
My fingers grasp it oh so close
Of its merits I often boast,

I use it driving in my car
Don't care where other drivers are,
It informs me of all matters
Facebook page and twitter chatter,

By chance while driving you come close
I'm doing what I love the most,
With steering wheel and cell in hand
My mind is lost -- in texting land!

Life's Quest

How is it that I've spent my life
With toils and tenderness?
At times I'd feast and then I'd fast
Not knowing things I missed,

How could I have knowingly
Turned a naked eye?
To all which has surrounded me
I let it slip right by,

In all my naked sorrows
In all my hopes and dreams,
How is it that I missed the point
Of life and all its dreams?

Was I clothed in ashes?
Was I draped in dreams?
Was I filled with sorrow
Of all my inner screams?

Why have I tomorrow?
Why have I today?
To make my dreams all borrowed?
Is life to be this way?

At what point do I not falter
And finally see my way?
Perhaps I'll seek the father
Who knows all end of days.

Life's Rudder

Lifeless do we wander
From sun to setting sun,
Giving minor ponder
To what we think we've won,

In all of our fulfillment
Or best of realized dreams,
In all of our achievements
Our structures and our themes,

We rarely think to wonder
Could any of this be?
A time to prove my stature
In what I cannot see,

If life is all but over
As soon as we are born,
If dying is our future
As from the womb we're torn,

If days we have are numbered
And soon will come to end,
If judged are we of treatment
To foe and of our friend,

Then how can we not fathom
That each and every day,
Our acts do give direction
To all along the way,

Our words take on new meaning
For when e'er spoke, they're born
They live a life thereafter
They're never from us torn,

Good or bad they persist
By all who have yet heard,
Yet seldom do we realize
Such life is in a word,

As in our beginning
When God created man,
A word created nature
And from there all God's plan,

And though considered perfect
With bound and bridled tongue,
Mere mortal man has yet to
Make perfect, all that's sung.

The Message

In our place, within our time
Soft-spoken moments, lines full of rhyme,
Every heartbreak, each daunted day
Comes with a price in which we all pay,

Earning a lesson which fills earthen souls
It conquers our essence and makes ourselves whole,
The lesson we find is true to the heart
Never to doubt it and from it not part,

Each shining moment in which we all live
Is precious to view and splendid to give,
That all of our essence and all of our lives
We keep pushing forward to end of our times,

So richly we are and blessed indeed
To live such a life inside eternity,
This message is for all who have read
And all who have heard - - both living and dead.

In Memory of
Yvette Michelle Preston
February 1, 1960 to May 13, 2015

The Mourning Light

Drip drop drip drop spatter splash
The rain came to the ground,
The air was cold, and earth was wet
With puddles all around,

In memories of all yesterdays
He sat and quietly thought,
Of lifelong friends and family
And treasures he had sought,

The air was filled with hint of spring
But he was old and dry,
His molted feathered wings gave out
He could no longer fly,

He looked up through the canopy
That shielded him from storm,
His talons old and wrinkly
In places a bit worn,

He barely moved to shun the drops
Of wetness from above,
His movements told of younger days
When life was full of love,

Then suddenly with bursting speed
He took into the air,
His stretched-out wings and feathers strong
He soared to where none dared,

With single thought and slightest twist
His path became anew,
He felt no wind resistance
As gracefully he flew,

The air was warm the sky was bright
With golden hints of hues,
The storm had passed, and all was fair
And easily to do,

The strength he once thought long since passed
Seemed but a breath away,
He flew as fast as thinking thought
Throughout half the day,

He landed with his talons strong
And then he looked and saw,
His body that was yesterday
Atop a heap of straw,

Then suddenly as dawning day
He felt a surge within,
His body took again to flight
And sailed within the wind,

He understood the passing storm
And why the sky was bright,
His spirit took its maiden flight
Within the mourning light.

Observance

Have you ever stopped to wonder?
Have you ever stopped to think?
That in all our joyous seasons
In which we feast in drink,

The newest celebration
The first day of the year,
We celebrate its coming
With champagne, song and beer,

Then woeful celebration
Honoring the man,
Who fought for civil freedoms
For all within this land,

And of our nation's father
Who took a formal stand,
Against hold from a country
In far off distant land,

The next day that we cheer for
Is a lover's holiday,
With chocolates and flowers
With great fortunes we will pay,

Then memory of soldiers
Who died within the field,
Their sacrifice for freedom
We celebrate and yield,

And of our independence
With rockets in the sky,
We ring aloud our anthem
To every passerby,

Then of the labor unions
We make it known to all,
We honor their achievements
And mark the coming fall,

Of Christopher Columbus
We mark this special day,
That when he finally landed
On this land USA,

All Hallows Eve is honored
With candy tricks and treats,
Our children with their costumes
Walk up and down the streets,

Then we hail all soldiers
Who served on every shore,
Their honorful commitment
To make this nation more,

Then our nation's thankful
Of pilgrims in strange lands,
When fathers of this nation
Made peace with native man,

Christ's day finally cometh
In which we spend in glee,
Honoring with presents
To all we know and see,

Of all these days here mentioned
Great advertisements flow,
That we should spend or borrow
And to the sales we go,

Yet in our splurging moments
We often fail to see,
The holiday's true meaning
Of what it's meant to be,

We glamorize the spending
We take a time of rest,
Forgetting the day's meaning
Which honored all our best.

Perverse Pride

To each his own a life for each
We gird our souls so none can teach,

We tell ourselves we know it all
So, none can dare to make us fall,

Our spirits high our ethics low
Our praise to God goes with the flow,

In God We Trust our motto grand
Yet we refuse all his command,

Commandments ten or so we're told
The greatest of - the rule of gold,

Of love to God to give our all
Of neighbors' heart to hear its call,

And yet we stray we compromise
To none offend - to none deny,

The Sodomites in years of old
Were yet the same and of it bold,

The sins they sought were of their own
Refused to hear of God's throne,

When angels stood near these men
Of them they would commit more sin,

A simple touch, - they could not see
Of the wrath, they could not flee,

No mercy shown to those within
That boldly took upon that sin,

Yet here today we think God changed
Of his will he re-arranged!

Because we sin, we think it right
That God will honor, us in that plight,

Oh, the madness! - Oh, the shame!
To think that God would re-arrange,

And make it naught of blood and cross
As sinful souls ignore the cost,

Of loving heart God stayed his hand
To a section of that land,

When his friend asked of heart
To save his kin from woeful part,

Here today where is the friend?
Whose hearts with God until the end?

Who then can cry to save a soul?
Who then can pray a different goal?

If I should think that God would change
And of his will to rearrange,

Then God would be just in my mind
Not maker of - - all things and time!

Pharaoh, Priest, or King

Solemn movements of the hand
Giving life to helms demands,
Making sculptures of desire
Making dreams of man transpire,

Always listening for the change
That our lives will re-arrange,
Giving space for needed stance
Our hearts and minds do e'er romance,

Voting for the man of hour
Hoping he will yield the power,
To give our hearts the needed try
To prove his worth in by and by,

We toil from dawn to ending dusk
We give our lives in that we must,
We seek to be free from the toil
That holds us bound to earthly soil,

In every inch of mile, we make
It seems that life will undertake,
The measure we have thought to won
Then proven we have passed no one,

Our hearts to see what comes to pass
And know that none is gained at last,
We seek to make another stance
And in our hearts, we e'er romance,

To place a soul of our desire
To make a sense of life's bogged mire,
We vote to sell our inner dream
In what will be one's inner scheme,

Not knowing of this self-desire
We lift this soul just one plane higher,
We say to self, "this one is us"
Not knowing of their inner fuss,

We say, "we'll win this campaign goal
It's what we need to be quite whole,"
But when all the voting's done
And our champ of life has won,

We find that none of change has past
And we're at where we were at last,
And all promises that made
Fall swiftly to a grave,

Then again, we rally, sing
Praises to a fore-born king,
One that never e'er will be
In this life of all we see,

But instead, we take the chance
That our hearts will e'er romance,
That of praises we will sing
Of a Pharaoh, Priest, or King.

Questions

Who are we that walk the Earth
And sail the seven seas?
We roam the skies and heavens vast
Our interests to appease,

What is the purpose of this time
In which we spend our thoughts?
As lips and ears do see and hear
Of what our eyes have caught?

Whence come we that speak of life
And seek the meaning of?
Have we come from earth beneath
Or heaven up above?

And speaking of earth whence came it from
And how long will it stand?
Are we really here by chance
Or was it made for man?

Whither do we go from here?
Where is it we will be?
Perhaps in time shall we know
All heaven's mysteries,

Could it be that by mistake
Fate has us therein?
Or could there be a supreme goal
That somehow, we might win?

The Reaching Heart

Love is such a feeling
Which tugs the tender heart,
It reaches in and grabs the soul
And does not wish to part,

It makes the heart so heavy
When distance is a bar,
Our thoughts do wander yonder
To those who are afar,

Our minds are filled with wishes
Of those we in heart hold,
To be with them is to us
A treasure good as gold,

We wonder why that with them
Our presence cannot be,
And why each fleeting moment
Seems an eternity,

We seek to be united
Each day in which we live,
Our hearts to melt together
And to each other give.

Resonance

What sounds we hear of nation's tribes
Of warring youthful men,
The cries of life – the tears of death
The anguish deep within,

What goals have we that walk the earth?
To kill what we don't know?
To exact death on sinless souls?
It's but a senseless goal,

What purity do we forget?
To know the master's plan?
To keep our brethren safe from harm?
To guide his feeble hand?

What love is lost of life we know?
That we should welcome death?
Have we fallen far from grace?
That life's a living test?

What chore is done or deed in heart
Do we now comprehend?
That takes us to the crimson flow
Where life both starts and ends?

Have we been taught to hurt ourselves?
And of the souls of man?
Or were we not of God's command
To uplift every man?

Where will we go? – What will we do?
To gain the supreme goal?
Can we find our way back
To that, that makes us whole?

Is living such a mystery
That we can't find its truth?
Or dying just an art to see
That there we see life's roots?

Can we in time if it persists
Find meaning in a breath?
Or will we want till last breath dawn
And never know our best?

Is it time we answer
The call that God once gave?
Who sent his son's salvation
To save us from the grave,

Can we find the opportune
To say 'No Way' to sin?
To praise the lord for light of day
And worship him within?

Can troubled times and heartfelt woes
Be stricken from our eyes?
Can love unfeigned and hearts unlocked
Be of our binding ties?

Can e'er we find the innocence
That comes from God above?
Can we trust with competence
And prove his way of love?

In time perhaps we all will see
The errors of our ways,
But given time is on us now
To change within our days,

If all we see and all we know
Is sorrow and of grief,
Then long's forgotten's Christ's blood flow
That gave our souls release.

The Search

Looking for that someone
I know that they can be,
The one that has my interests
The one that interests me,

The less am I without them
My life is standing still,
I really can't be doubt-full
This person must be real,

I pray that if you're out there
Don't hesitate to say,
"I too was looking for you
Be in my life today"

So be that someone special
That makes life so fulfilled,
With every smiling gesture
Of purest heart instilled.

The Story

The witness as he sees it
A gift of sight to hold,
To see the makes of time vent
The story to unfold,

The story is of magic
To those who understand,
Or perhaps it's of tragic
To every righteous man,

The story may be fulfilled
Or perhaps misery,
It can be of a night's tale
Of how it came to be,

Any way it's measured
The story can be told,
In differing viewpoints
Until the story's sold.

Techie Santa

If Santa had a spaceship
He'd fly so very fast,
The kids would barely notice
His sleigh as he would pass,

The toys would be so techie
The list would be so large,
His spaceship would resemble
A red large floating barge,

Instead of using reindeer
His plasma jets would haul,
Our fastest flying airplanes
Would seem to him a crawl,

Instead of milk and cookies
Of what we know he ate,
The kids would be more thoughtful
And leave for him nitrate,

If Santa had a spaceship
Instead of using elves,
His toys would be so stellar
We'd ask for one ourselves!

Slumbering Dreams

in every dreaming moment
we wish for inner things
in the slothful slumber
and the rest that it brings

we wish to e'er be humble
in our truest scheme
we wish for bright tomorrows
when waking from the dream

but dreams aren't always pleasant
as we'd have them be
sometimes they're a nightmare
as dreams can often be

dreams are from the inside
they tell us what we fear
dreams are from the outside
in colors that are clear

dreams are filled with sorrow
dreams are filled with hate
dreams are filled with hoping
dreams are filled with fate

dreams can be of magic
dreams can be dreamed late
dreams can be of sadness
dreams can irritate

dreams can be of wishing
of what we do not have
dreams can be of knowing
of what we cannot grab

dreaming of tomorrows
or dreaming of the past
dreams can be quite fleeting
or seem to ever last

dreams can be of waking
from our slumbered state
dreams can be of making
our inner self debate

dreams can be of fortune
dreams can be of fame
dreams can be of people
in which we cannot name

if dreams become our refuge
from our thoughts within
and nighttime is our teacher
of what the dream can win

then dreaming of the future
or dreaming of the past
is just our conscious saying
it's just a dream - - at last!

Toil

Each morning that we rise
We have a vision of,
Things we need to do that day
Things that we hate and love,

Whenever we prepare to work
We seek to do our best,
To look and feel to play the part
Let fate sort out the rest,

Our journeyed day begins on wake
We start with thoughts preparing,
We give ourselves time to adjust
Our minds and hearts forbearing,

When 'ere we finally break the morn
We start our tasks that beg,
With fervor lasting till the dusk
We strive to get ahead,

Once a single task completes
Another takes its place,
It's like a marathon of life
We cannot win this race,

Hours pass and minutes drag
We conquer and we fail,
Again, we try till set complete
As end of day sets sail,

Through our lives we run this race
With our lives we live it,
In any case it is a chore
Daily--our all we give it,

When day e'er ends we look back
We see our strengths and goals,
We measure life by what we've done
Not by what we're told,

From birth to death this cycle turns
Repeating every hour,
Our lives we live and that which we give
Derives of divine power,

When once we look at life to see
We're more than what we do,
With joy we know what we can be
And what will guide us through,

When what our hands have found to do
Is done as unto God,
Disdain and slack we will eschew
Our ethics we will rod,

Our dreams our goals our victories
All are all within our grasp,
When once we look to things not past
And work toward that at last.

To Those Who Serve

From all of us we wish to say
We're thankful that you served,
With open hearts we give today
It's less than you deserve,

Your sacrifice for us to live
With freedoms that we share,
You gave more than just your time
It's much for you to bear,

The season is upon us now
To seek to you to give,
The joys that fate would not allow
And to those of whom you live,

With pride you served your country
With courage you fought fates end,
You're more to us than you can see
You're family, our hearts, our friends.

We Are

In times of pitied sorrow
We seek to know life's goal,
Are we here for the tomorrow?
Is our science true as told?

Will e'er we know why we're living
Here on earth our island grand,
Do we know who holds tomorrow?
Do we know the future's plan?

Not for pity or for sorrow
Not for love of every man,
Not for planning for tomorrow
Not for wars in every land,

Not for greed or wealthy gaining
Not for paupers' empty hands,
But the slight of our existence
Twas the voice of God's command.

The Winds of Change

The winds of change are blowing
With lofty softly breeze,
While we are ever growing
To meet this change with ease,

Sometimes we find our virtue
Is in the changing wind,
Sometimes we find our statues
Are where the wind begins,

As we mature in lifetime
We know each change we see,
But changes that the wind makes
Are changed so subtly,

Although the changes welcomed
We fear what we can't see,
The future of the changes
The winds that make them be,

Our future's never certain
If winds will blow at all,
But instead, we hold on steadfast
Till we hear the wind's change call,

The changes of tomorrow
Are the futures of today,
We meet them without sorrow
For these winds will guide our way.

Undertow

In this life of love and laughter
Daily worries, fears, and woes,
We plan to live in God's hereafter
Seeking faith and What God knows,

Daily we find all distractions
From the goal we first set forth,
Troubled times and forceful laughter
Paths that take us from the course,

In our heart of hearts in reason
We may find a troubled past,
Blinding us from the vision
Faith had given us to last,

Peter walked upon the water
Then his faith began to doubt,
His sinking soul in waters raging
To the savior gave a shout,

Of faith we know there is tomorrow
And yet our eyes just see today,
Do we know our God and savior
Has purchased our entire way?

Do we let our daily tortures
Keep us from his spirit grand?
Do we let our inner being
Keep our faith in sinking sand?

Do we know that all tomorrows
Are held by him that made the day?
Do we know that troubled sorrows
Lend to faith to change the way?

Is it sadness, is it anger
Of our faults, our fears, our doubts,
Is it of all unseen danger
Of what we fear we'll live without?

What keeps us from the triumphed victory?
Given once to redeemed lost,
What hides from that hallowed sanctuary?
Bought with Christ upon the cross?

Is it that our fears of reason
Keep our hearts from truthful ties?
Hindering us from all redemption
Of the cross where victory lies?

Shall we stay within this blunder?
Knowing that our Lord did rise,
Or shall we cast all doubts asunder
And reign with God in heaven's skies?

To What End?

To What end is all the madness
That compasses us round?
To what end is all the sadness
That follows evil's sound?

To what end is all the preaching
If no one cares to hear?
To what end is teaching loving
If no one is held dear?

A solitary madness
A man with jilted gun,
The n becomes the sadness
Of those who could not run,

A moment suicidal
Which takes more than the one,
And ends a life so fragile
Yet madness isn't done,

The lawmakers are calling
To screen the hardened souls,
Not let them yield a weapon
To them it can't be sold,

What end is all the violence
That newsrooms make to shine?
Instead of viewing victims
The perk gets light of lime,

To what end is the reason
That peace patrols do fear?
Of dangers that they can't see
From those who shed no tear?

What end is there of sorrow
Of loved ones lost to crime?
Will we see tomorrow?
Will we have more time?

Words

Words, Words
All around,
They make us smile
They make us frown,

They soar our strength
They teach to fly,
We read at length
From birth to die,

We seek to know
We seek to share,
We seek to judge
We seek to care,

Words of speech
Of signs of hand,
Words in text
In virtual land,

Words in a song
A poem that rhymes,
Words in a book
That tethers time,

Words that we know
Words that perplex,
With words we all grow
To what we'll be next,

Not one word spoken
Is truer than,
Words that compel
The heart of man.

The Wrestler

The move, the bend, the wrap-around
The angle and the mat,
The time it takes to find a way
To pin the shoulders flat,

The ref's quick eye and whistle
The hand slap to the floor,
The audience's wrestle
The feel "I could do more"

From every twisted angle
From every parent's dream,
To honored medal's dangle
To winners' circle scene,

I choose to do the wrestle
Not for parents' pride,
But rather of what nestles,
In heart -- and in my stride.

Calvary

As we see our world today
In merits of its birth,
We understand by faith was framed
This world and all it's worth,

If by faith, we know for sure
All creation stands,
Then by same were certain of
The life of Christ and man,

By faith we know that Christ was born
To save us from our sin,
By faith we know his flesh was torn
By faithlessness of men,

By faith we know that every lash
That tore his flesh away,
Were lashes that brought healing
To all who kneel and pray,

By faith we know his wounds
About his body whole,
Took away transgressions
From body and our soul,

By faith we know his bruises
Hide our iniquities,
By faith we know salvation
He gave to you and me,

He took upon a world of sin
That was not his own,
To give the freedom to all men
To see him on his throne,

By faith we know the truth of things
That the bible tells,
By faith we see it in our hearts
And in our mind, it shelves,

Yet every time we tell a lie
Or have a lustful thought,
Or say a word from passions depth
At our emotions cost,

Every time we abstain from
What the spirit bids,
Every time we shun the poor
Refusing there to give,

Again, we bruise we wound we lash
At crucifixions lot,
Denying holy sacrifice
Give honor to it not,

Every time we cheat or steal
We place another lash,
Every time from flesh we feel
We repeat Golgotha's past,

The cost of our salvation
For Christ – his life was lost,
Redeeming us from worldly sin
So, love would be our cost,

We pray unto God's spirit
Through faith within his son,
Keeping our hearts near it
For all victories ever won,

Daily taking treasure
In membrance of the cross,
Denying fleshly pleasure
Preaching to the lost,

Living for the savior
Who died and rose for all,
Seeking to be the hearer
To answer spirit's call,

If by our words and all our deeds
We seek the praise of God,
And by our thoughts and inner dreams
We seek approving nod,

Then daily Calvary's meaning
From us is never lost,
But deep within is burning
Our savior and our cross.

Distant

How far have we come today?
How far have we fallen?
Have we lost the guarded way?
Have we lost our calling?

Is there time to find anew
The path that we must take?
Is there time to meet the groom
Whom waits at heaven's gate?

Shall we ever stop to see
The distance that we've lost?
Can it change or to e'er be
The heavy shameful cost?

When will we finally turn to know
The errors in our past?
And make the future sure to flow
With God's eternal cast?

How often do we stop and pray
To thank God for the day?
When e'er do we kneel to say
"God lead me in your way?"

Perhaps in time if life permits
All mysteries will be known,
But if by chance we're called today
Would we see his throne?

To God be all the glory
For God be all the praise,
In God be all the worship
By God we live our days.

Draw Me

Draw me near to thee oh Lord
Draw me near to thy side,
Draw me near to thee oh Lord
In thy spirit to abide,

Lord, I ask and Lord I pray
Keep me close don't let me stray,
Lord, I praise oh Lord I sing
To thou eternal oh Lord and King,

Lord keep my heart and make it soft
Keep it with you aloft,
Lord keep my mind oh keep my soul
That I may forever be made whole,

Oh lord I pray you hear me now
Draw me e'er close don't let me down,
Keep me high within your love
As I praise you God above.

Echo

Shining, twinkling in night's sky
These dots above our heads,
Celestial marvels far and wide
These stars in heaven's stead,

Our galaxy of very old
Never has once turned,
This Milky Way as seen in sight
A name of which it earned,

Yet not alone and there is kin
Of which it shares great space,
The universe holds billions more
And some that seem to race,

As we spin in our space
Our view becomes more clear,
We see more lights within its hold
We see both far and near,

Pulsars, quasars, comets
Nebula, planets, moons,
Deep black space, dense bright stars
The grandeur's greatness looms,

Scientific study
Tells us how it's made,
How gravity formed Earth
Of some planets waylaid,

We speak of Earth's beginning
Of how all stars will end,
We speak of black holes winning
Of what all space can send,

We think we know the reason
Of how all planets formed,
Of what makes dark and sunlight
Of celestial bodies born,

Yet do we know the reason
Of what we see at night?
Perhaps it's just the echo
Of words - - "Let there be light..."

Eternity & Time

Years I've walked through life
And felt myself alone,
Seeking greater meaning
And looking to God's throne,

Years I've often wondered
When would be the day?
That all my sorrows parted?
And bliss would come my way?

Often times I sat and thought
What means is to this end?
What is it am I here to do?
What part of life I'll win?

Sometimes it seems that all has brought
Me to this serene thought,
Perhaps my life is meant to be
So others may be free,

In Antioch the Christians there
Were said to act like Christ,
And yet he loved one e'er so dear
Yet he denied him thrice,

If all my hopes and dreams were true
And every moment mine,
This life would be so meaningless
To everyone I find,

If Christ gain all the glory
And yet bore all the pain,
What in life can stop me now
From serving him again?

Since all I find within me
Is what I've come to bear,
All I have to do is ask
Do I really want it there?

Life is such a mystery
We never know tomorrow,
And all we really know for sure
Is that we don't like sorrow,

Yet sorrows seem to find us
And then we seek to pray,
That nothing ever binds us
From God's most perfect way,

Yet Christ is ever giving
And calling us to ask,
In faith in him believing
He will perform the task,

All we have and what we are
Is simply his design,
And victory for all he gave
For Eternity --- & Time!

The Gift

A prayer when I was younger
To write unto God's name,
Not of tears of sorrow
Nor of mindless fame,

The writing that I sought so
Was to the depth of soul,
The tender and the spirit
Of what would make one whole,

The words of never ending
To sound within oneself,
Of what the spirit needed
To mend as it was helped,

To open fastened portals
Within the heart of man,
To speak of spirit wisdom
As pertains to God's plan,

This gift of which I asked for
Would never seem to age,
And the works of the completeness
Before pen touched to page,

The unction of the spirit
To author every line,
Then give God the glory
Of what truly isn't mine,

This gift that I asked for
Was unto every man,
To know that all tomorrows
Were solely in God's hands.

God's Soliloquy

God said "Let there be light"
Our Sun was born that day,
Days began and spurned the night
Since – time has come to stay,

Once again God's voice is heard
Whereof not by man,
Nature hears and sprouts to life
So, this time Earth began,

Outer darkness turned to lights
Lighting the night's sky,
In paraphrasing why they're there
"Lights to plant crops by"

Our nature's truest meanings
Question as to why,
Until we find the reason
Yahweh framed the skies,

To gain for him a family
Of which we are a part,
United all together
Sprung from God's own heart.

In God's Eyes

In God's eyes all are children
In God's eyes we have not yet grown,
In God's eyes there is no sorrow
In God's eyes our sins we don't own,

In God's eyes there is no malice
In God's eyes there is no hate,
In God's eyes there is no fear
In God's eyes death does not take,

In God's eyes there is no pigment
In God's eyes there is no debate,
In God's eyes there is freedom
In God's eyes there is no ill fate,

In God's eyes all are equal
In God's eyes our spirits are seen,
In God's eyes his love is e'er lasting
In God's eyes if we could only believe,

In God's eyes just one look
Could open our eyes to eternity's stand,
And through his eyes our childish behavior
Could finally be thwarted and yield his command,

In God's eyes we are but children
In our eyes, we are but man.

I Prayed a Prayer

I prayed a prayer
It filled the room with sounds of hope's despair
I felt it consume me with deep care
On bended knees,
With hands raised high,
I prayed a prayer

I prayed a prayer
I felt God's holy spirit everywhere
The majesty of heaven took my care
On bended knees,
With hands raised high,
I prayed a prayer

I prayed a prayer
I prayed to be much better than I've been
I prayed that God would keep my soul from sin
On bended knees,
With hands raised high,
I prayed a prayer

I prayed a prayer
I asked of God for burdens I could bear
To clear the path for folks out there somewhere
On bended knees,
With hands raised high,
I prayed a prayer

I prayed a prayer
To help me understand what all I see
To help me do what God would ask of me
On bended knees,
With hands raised high,
I prayed a prayer

I prayed a prayer
And asked of God to never let me go
To keep my inner thoughts on him e'er so
On bended knees,
With hands raised high,
I prayed a prayer...

On bended knees,
With hands raised high,
I prayed a prayer...

Latter Rain

Some years ago, I stood I praised
I raised my hands held high,
I worshipped God's entirety
I felt his spirit nigh,

In all of my surroundings whole
I parted from the sounds,
Of the people standing near
I stood on hallowed ground,

I lifted voice and yelled aloud
To God alone I cried,
And then it happened suddenly
My spirit came untied,

Softly splashing on my skin
I felt his spirit dear,
It brought an overwhelming peace
Unknown in all my years,

His spirit softly raised my soul
To such a peaceful place,
The silence there with air of praise
I felt his spirit's grace,

Upon my lips I felt a splash
It loosened voice and tongue,
I felt a great euphoria
My natural feelings numb,

It splashed my eyes and top of head
It splashed my whole of being,
Then all I knew was sweet release
And by his spirit seeing,

Then to God bowed myself
To worship him and praise,
Adoring spirit ever so
For all my living days,

Then I heard the elders praise
The twenty and the four,
They fell to knee to worship God
For now, and evermore,

To all who've known this feeling past
Within this place of praise,
I offer just a single thought
Of memory to raise,

This feeling that enraptured me
And shook my whole of frame,
Was God descending on my soul
His spirit's Latter Rain.

The Lord

The Lord is great and righteous
His spirit ever free,
He comes to us so softly
We often do not see,

The Lord is great and mighty
His hands do always care,
He guides us with his presence
His spirit's everywhere,

The Lord is great and magnified
His kingdom never ends,
He calls to us from heaven
He calls to us as friends.

Lord, I Ask

Lord, I ask you heal my eyes
That your will I do see,
Let me praise you ever deep,
Sincere continually,

Lord, I ask you heal my ear
To listen to your voice,
To give you all you'll ever ask
To make that my life's choice,

Lord, I ask you heal my mind
So, I may understand,
That you are Lord, the King of all,
On Earth in every land,

Lord, I ask you heal my heart
So, hatred cannot be,
That I embrace your lovingness
From now till eternity,

Lord, I ask you hear my prayer
That I may feel you near,
And at the alter leave my cares
And there lay all my fears,

Lord, I ask you touch me now
And wake my sleeping soul,
As I surrender all I am
And from my ails be whole,

Lord, I ask with open heart
And peace and joy within,
To know you more than yesterday
Escaping worldly sin,

Lord, I ask to ask no more
Of what I feel I need,
But give you all I ever was
And all I'll ever be.

Lost

Too far away I've traveled from home
Forsaking first love while aimless I roam,
Not knowing the truth of all of my days
Not knowing the love that never will stray,

I find I am lost with nowhere to hide
I find I am cursed with thorns in my side,
My troubles agree that I'm doomed in my life
My days are of sin and meaningless strife,

A turn for the worse is coming ahead
My body grows weak my spirit grows dead,
If I should but turn and look toward the prize
My woes will all stop, and I'll open my eyes,

The master has called he's opened the door
His spirit says come and live evermore,
He calls to our souls to answer his voice
He gives to us all the eternal choice.

On Bended Knee

On bended knee and needful prayer
We make our pleas to God,
Our thoughts, our hopes, our wishes
Where men and angels trod,

We seek to know more meaning;
We fall to God to pray,
With stammered lips and kneeling
We seek the words to say,

Do we pray for mercy?
Healing or of wealth?
Do we pray for others?
Family or of health?

Do we ask in wisdom?
Or do we ask in vain?
Do we pray of child faith?
Or repeat prayer again?

Do we pray in circles?
In that we would be known?
Do we pray to God's heart?
To be called his own?

Do we pray of lust of eye?
Which is the same as act?
Do we pray of what makes faith?
To know it is a fact?

Do we pray to God on high?
Or to our inner self?
Do we pray throughout the day?
Or after first prayer shelf?

Do we pray to meet a goal?
Of flesh and of desire?
Do we pray to become whole?
To lift our spirit higher?

Have we yet encountered
The reasons for all prayer?
To know our hearts desire
And leave all sinning there?

Do we know the depth of prayer?
And understand its toll?
That bruises, thorns, and blood of Christ
Clean spirit of the soul?

Do we come to God as bold?
Or softly due to sin?
Do we pray in faith's belief?
That by our prayers we win?

Do we know that all our thoughts?
Do edify or tear?
Do we know that in our heart
Always we're in prayer?

On bended knee and needful prayer
We pray to God alone,
Do we know he hears us?
And our prayers reach his throne?

Perhaps we'll find the answers
Upon our bended knee,
Perhaps well see all answered
With Christ at Calvary.

On to Prayer

On to prayer I kneel to thee
Seeking what I need to be,
Yielding all to you at last
Letting go my habits past,

On to prayer I worship thee
Letting my life's minions flee,
Holding fast to your love true
Accepting all you said you'll do,

On to prayer I see at last
The mold of which I have cast,
Openly I call to thee
For you have set my spirit free,

Jesus Christ to you I pray
I may endure just one more day,
With open heart I seek your face
That I may know your spirit's grace.

Out From Among Them

Out of the mire, out of the throws
Out of the outcast, out of the woes,
Out from the clearings, so ever dry
Out of the sheerings, out of the cries,

Out of the wastelands, out of the dire
Out of the turmoils and all that transpires,
Out of the darkness and into the light
Into God's love and out of the fight,

Into the splendid, into the love
Into the wonders, that come from above,
Into the daylight, and out of the night
Into the Son's light, and out of the fright,

Into the blessings, into the word
Into the calling that I once have heard,
Forever giving of all that I am
To God's own pleasure, to honor the lamb.

Tender Mercies

To the Lord my love I give
And all my life for him I'll live,
His love has kept my soul from sin
Then he cleansed my heart within,

He watches me through day and night
When the devil tries to fight,
His angels watch and keep my ground
For in his heart a place I've found,

He leads me to his place of praise
And fills my soul with love he gave,
His eyes on me my heart on him
This world of sorrow has grown quite dim,

He gives to me such liberty
My heart within can now be free,
His songs of praise do touch my lips
His bleeding side upon me drips,

He gave his life to save my soul
My life to him I give in whole,
His spirit bids "Come unto me
That you may live eternally."

The Perfect Heart

Where is your faith when the daylight goes wrong?
And where is your love when it fails?
Where is the light when the moonbeams are gone?
Have they all taken flight or sailed?

How many times have you looked up and prayed?
And how many times have you praised?
Love is much more than the phrase we all say
It's heights and its depths are grayed,

Higher than mountains, it's there I am told
Lower than valleys, it's more precious than gold,
It's more than a word from our lips to our ears
It's part of our God - - - Throughout space and years,

Folk try to tell you that your life is all wrong
Yet you know the truth is tied in a song,
It's a song that you sing with praise on your lips
And a truth that you've known
Through life's worst eclipse,

Christ is much nearer than we often know
He left a great message telling us so,
Just one prayer to him with faith in our heart
Makes miracles happen, - - and storm clouds depart,

Life is e'er growing and we always learn
Sometimes we are failing, but Grace we can't earn,
It's given so freely from Jesus above
And the reason he died was to give us his love,

"Oh lord I do falter and find that I sin
I feel I'm not perfect and torn deep within,
But knowing your Grace lord has lifted me high
To know that your perfect - - and never am I."

The Pew

There in the pulpit out in the pew
Worries are many and troubles not few,
Somehow the message is dwindling away
As prayer warriors stumble to pray,

Often we hear of the troubles we have
Pressing our conscious and blocking the lamb,
Taking our victory and casting away
The truth that God's word has to say,

Over and over and over again
We hold to the promise and let go of sin,
The cycle continues each time that we meet
Our worries we lay at Christ's feet,

How would it be if somehow someday
We let go of worries and troubles abate?
We live in his promise proclaiming the faith
And realize upon him we wait?

Gladly we'd praise him raising our hearts
Our spirits cry loudly as his love imparts,
Our hopes and fears become praises and cheers
As victory lives in our years.

The Prayer

Yester eve a prayer I prayed
It stammered from my lips,
I prayed for all the sinful souls
To find the love that lifts,

I prayed for those of misfortune
Whom do not know a home,
That they may find a kindred soul
And never more to roam,

I prayed for orphaned children
And widows of their mate,
I prayed they all find comfort
I prayed this not be late,

I prayed for those whom loved ones
Had passed on from this life,
I prayed that of their sorrow
Be shadows dimmed by light,

I prayed that nations warriors
Be withdrawn from the field,
I prayed that every battle
Henceforth to cease and yield,

I prayed for all the clergy
To fall unto their knees,
And think not of their future
But unto God to please,

I prayed that all the nations
Upon this planet grand,
Give heed unto God's spirit
And to his voiced command,

I prayed for all the loved ones
Whom passed far from this life,
Find peace within God's spirit
Whom knows their fated plight,

I prayed for the starving
Those in the cold or heat,
To be upon men's burdens
And of their needs to meet,

I prayed that all tomorrows
Be blessed of yesterday,
As we all find the wisdom
To kneel to God to pray,

Yesterday I prayed a prayer
Down on bended knee,
And asked of God it come to pass
This prayer was not for me,

I prayed for all the world to know
That God created man,
I prayed for love and lasting peace
In all nations and all lands,

Truly all tomorrows
Are formed from all todays,
Truly all of mankind
Can find much better ways,

Today again I pray a prayer
From my heart and mind,
I pray God's will upon us all
I pray for all mankind.

Purpose

In times of pitied sorrow
We seek to know life's goal,
Are we here for the morrow?
Is our science true as told?

Will e'er we know why we're living?
Here on earth our island grand,
Do we know who holds tomorrow?
Do we know the father's plan?

Not for pity or for sorrow
Not for love of every man,
Not for planning for tomorrow
Not for wars in every land,

Not for greed or wealthy gaining
Not for pauper's empty hands,
But the start of our existence
Twas the voice of God's command.

Revelation

All your years of days gone by
All your learning past,
Is summed up in one remark
Of what will always last,

Not of visions, not of dreams
Not of things not seen,
Not of all you've learned; you saw
Not what could have been,

All you've learned and all you know
Has brought you to your knees,
There you've found an answer true
That flesh will not appease,

There is one who holds all keys
All knowledge future; past,
He holds our lives within his heart
With him we will e'er last.

Righteous Echo

Hours pass and days go by
Time goes speeding on,
Storms of thunder overcast
And that we gaze upon,

Through our lives we look we seek
Of what will ever last,
Hoping that a dream is real
Our wanting goal surpass,

We hold on to our loved ones
We hang on to our past,
We raise our children slowly
In hopes their time e'er lasts,

We seek our education
We save for futures end,
We daily make our pardons
We reach out to our friends,

In all our constant living
Within our daily grind,
When do we seek the savior?
Who granted us this time?

Which prayer does part our lips so
That praises follow on?
Which verse does grab our heart so
Our soul will carry on?

Do we forget to honor
Our God who made us so?
Do we forget to know that
It's he who makes us grow?

Do we forget our true selves
Of which we have thus come?
Do we forget the master
Of whom all life comes from?

Perhaps a prayer of mending
May humble us in his eyes,
Perhaps our praise ascending
Will make our spirits rise,

Perchance we make the savior
More than story told,
We'd finalize life's chapters
With God's own heart in hold.

Salvation's Theme

Years ago, a savior hang
While nailed onto a tree,
He bled his blood and felt his pain
To set the sinful free,

Every drop that dripped that day
Cleansed from man a sin,
His inward self he gave to us
To make us pure within,

His thoughts of man throughout time
Would not let this cup pass,
For every sin he bled that day
This was his lifelong task,

Though a mighty savior
Is Christ to you and me,
When there he hang the people sang
"Of him we are now free",

We know he is the Lord of Lords
Is grand in all respects,
We love him awely in our hearts
And go as he directs,

His love so great was proved that hour
He's Lord, yes Lord of hosts,
Now angels sing and choirs praise
Of him all heaven boasts,

Yet torn in heart was he that day
Thorns pleated in his head,
His back yet raw as butchers grind
His face was bloodstain red,

Such a torment people say
How awful had it been,
Yet they themselves repeat these acts
Each time they choose to sin,

Christ the king and lord of lords
Calls to all mankind,
"Acknowledge me with all your heart
And I will make you mine."

Spirit

Today I woke and fumbled through
The thoughts within my head,
As I sorted through the dreams I had
While laying on my bed,

I thought of times I've often seen
And memories of your smile,
I thought of hope and endless dreams
I lay and thought awhile,

When I stirred from my place
I looked unto God's sky,
The puffy clouds and crystal sky
Soared my spirit high,

I felt the awesomeness of God
Of hopes, of dreams, of power,
And wondered at his slandered grace
Through that remaining hour,

As time passed, I felt a breeze
Which swept throughout my soul,
I felt his sigh and pleasantness
And felt within, quite whole,

The trees, the flowers, birds, and air
All seemed to have God's touch,
My eyes saw God in everything
Then I felt loved so much,

All I'd seen and felt today
Cried loudly to my heart,
God has blessed me ever so
And has from my life's start,

In viewing all God's grand design
I realized one thing true,
He made all heavens and all Earth
To know both me and you,

For his pleasure were all things made
And his pleasure is but truth,
His pleasures were but all foretold
As in the book of Ruth,

Forsaking all our ties which bind
And hold us to this Earth,
To birth in spirit to his love
And that of virgin birth,

For Christ was born of spirit
And now so much are we,
To know his love and truthfulness
While worries from us flee,

Our souls are captured in God's truth
And freed for once, for all,
To know that God alone has power
And false are satin's calls,

The beauty of this day you see
Is not just trees and flowers,
But understanding God's great love
And purpose of his powers,

His love he gives to you and me
Is without recompense,
And prices paid for all his works
Are solely his expense.

Tasking

Be mindful of the daily tasks
That make us who we are,
Be observant of things now and past
That keep us near and far,

This life is filled with mysteries
Of which we never learn,
And also filled with victories
Of which we seldom earn,

When e'er we live above reproach
We cleanse the soul within,
When we fail to be our most
We falter and we sin,

In days ahead we plan our lives
Of what we'll say and do,
But seldom does it hap that way
We strive to follow through,

For victory's sake and penance paid
We give from deep within,
Our hearts seek God as spirit guide
And to him we will blend,

Glory, honor and selfish pride
We seek and mar our soul,
Peace, and love with selfless stride
Will turn our souls yet whole,

All we do, we think, we say
Is felt both far and wide,
A thought once spoke gains life itself
From life it will not hide,

Every measure we may know
Is based on what we've learned,
God's plan for us is measured so
His plan we've yet to learn.

The Wonder of It All

We look, we reach, we live
Of our lives to God we give,
Others wanting spurs our ears
To listen for their hopes and fears,

We see the Earth and all its glory
Never knowing its full story,
Casting fears and doubts aside
We take a stand and will abide,

We see the stars tat shine so bright
With the moon they rule the night,
We hear the rustling of the wind
Not where it starts nor where it ends,

We seek the answers of the day
And yet forget it's when we pray,
That then and only will we see
How God made us and harmony,

Once a day we pray a prayer
In our hearts we know God's there,
And what our eyes do not behold
We treasure more than finest gold,

As the Earth spins day and night
As the nighttime fades to light,
As the seasons come and go
We forget what we should know,

We look, reach, and then we live
When we find that to others give,
The thing that we would have the most
Our hearts, our care, and of our boasts,

We see this life and all around
We have barely known the sound,
Of what the master's plan has called
Nor the wonder of it all.

Time's Essence

Each speck of time that's passing
Carries more than wind,
But all of our life's passing
Of friendships and our kin,

As time is all around us
It's more of life we see,
When time itself resounds us
We're more than we can be,

Of all our prayers and fastings
Our reach to be our best,
It's time that finally answers
Our answers to life's tests,

More than passing moments
More than days gone by,
Time is more than passing
But taking us on high,

Time will never falter
Nor fail to comprehend,
What God has set in motion
From start until time's end,

To God we give the glory
For moments that we spend,
In God's blessed story
That does not have an end,

On this special morning
And in this special day,
Let time simply guide you
To God who owns the way,

His blessings are enduring
His spirit ever strong,
His healing is forever
His reach is deep and long,

If time is as a vapor
In which we live our stand,
Then time will heed to answer
The voice of God's command.

Triumph of Silence

The scene is set -- the mood is hate;
A man in silence awaits his fate,
A jury grand of priests, they all
Are gathered in the judgment hall,

They see the man of whom they would
Destroy His soul, if only they could,
There is no defense on his behalf;
The governor joins their staff,

The room is filled with accusations;
The man stands still with utmost patience,
In scorn and laughter, in mockery they cry,
"This man blasphemed, by law should die!"

Yet silently, He stood and heard
All of their hate, yes, every word,
A judge was He of all creation
Of every man, of every nation,

His identity would not reveal;
But to them had He chosen to conceal,
For though He died upon the cross,
The triumph of silence did save the lost.

The Wanderer

Where we wander, where we go
Time will tell, time will know,
In this life we have listed
All our kin, all our misfit,

All our knowledge still remains
As sun turning stays the same,
It's our pleasure to be our all
It's our birthright to hear God's call,

When we leave this life our own
We shall know God at his throne,
Yet we merit our kinship nigh
We hold on and raise them high,

Giving place to all who read
Of our actions, of our deeds,
When at last we leave this life
We take our place in heaven's light.

Unmerited Favor

I used to think a debt I owe
So awesome and so great,
And how I could repay my God
Yes, what would be my fate?

But Jesus has revealed to me
That he has paid the price,
Even as he did that day
When Peter denied him thrice,

I am now free of the debt
That I could not repay,
And Jesus has so tenderly
Showed me a brand-new way,

To sing the songs of Zion
And live from day to day,
To sing and shout and even dance
With joy and love to enhance,

To praise God for the victory
For by his grace was given,
And to forever love him so
Every day I'm living.

We Rise

In essence of our nature
We pray the sinner's prayer,
We find the penitent alter
And cast our burdens there,

We seek not pitied sorrow
And we have none to blame,
Our past is there to die from
And rise in Jesus name,

We seek not for the morrow
We seek not golden coin,
We seek not things to borrow
But to Christ's spirit join,

We don't consider shameful
The life we leave behind,
We seek forever mindful
And of God's statutes mind,

We kneel at hallowed alter
And ask the spirit be,
Cleansed from sinful matters
And death from us to flee,

We cry unto the master
Who holds all natures plan,
We change our life filled chapter
To his voiced command,

We wrest this battle daily
To know his spirit true,
To feel his nod of pleasure
In what we say and do,

The beauty of salvation
Our raiment through God's eyes,
Is of our tortured savior
For by his blood - - we rise.

Where Angels Trod

In the dawning of all time
There is God who knows all minds,
Not of just the minds that be
But from dawn till eternity,

Every spirit not yet born
Is with God yet on that morn,
Every riddle, every rhyme
Every substance of all kind,

Celestial bodies in night's air
All our worries, all our cares,
Every day and night is born
In God's presence on that morn,

Time itself is in God's hand
As are oceans and all land,
The galaxies so far so vast
From God's presence are not cast,

Every star that ever shines
Is in God, in endless time,
From creation's bursting past
Till the dusk our time will last,

To God is all and all the same
For God of certain will not age,
The universe and time within
Are all in God, where all has been,

When God says "Let there be light"
He also shows of Samson's might,
And Israel crosses the dry Red Sea
And Christ walks shores of Galilee,

And wars are fought, and wars are won
And born to us is God's own son,
And nations born and nations die
And Christ betrayed is crucified,

And Noah's ark saves the world
And we boast of our flags unfurled,
We preach the kingdom of the cross
That Christ is here to save the lost,

God says to Adam and to Eve
"Multiply" - - To us; "believe,"
And all our future and our past
Within God has not one second passed,

For God sees present and all time
Within one single frame of mind,
God isn't bound or yoked by time
But all's in him, in him we find,

We can count our days of sin
But all creation, is of God in,
He knows every thought of mind
Of every soul throughout time,

He's on every strand of land
In all worlds, his voice commands,
All we ever hope to see
Dare to go or hope to be,

God is there and always been
And this creator calls us kin,
Every thought from minds of men
Cannot think where God's not been,

He's everywhere in every time
In every verse and every rhyme,
And all the same, he's without age
And found on every bible page,

For us to even understand
The might of God and his command,
We must give space that all we know
Is in God forever so,

To know this, heaven's host applaud
"They've come to know where angels trod!"
The knowledge that all space and time
Bears no difference in God's mind.

Yesterday, Today, and Victory

Yesterday I looked around
To see how far I've come,
And then today I asked the Lord
"Which way did I come from?"

I felt so lost within myself
I couldn't find my way,
In anguish I cried out to God
"Oh Lord please hear me pray!"

This pasture which I've placed myself
Has ever fading grass,
It's trodden down and eaten so
I know it will not last,

If I could just but find a gate
My soul would be set free,
To ever luscious grass that's green
My soul would ever feed,

Now grass which sets on other side
The greens are all the same,
But there I do not need to hide
And no one gets the blame,

But burdens are not fields of grass
They're weights unto the soul,
And sorrows are not made to last
But temporal I am told,

Yet I still look for openness
To free my weary heart,
Of pastures which will have no fence
My sorrows to depart,

I ask my Lord of where I've been
And how long will it be?
Till I feel I have made amends
And finally, I am free?

I ask one simple prayer my friend
When you think of me,
Just pray that I may find his will
And truth so splendidly,

Tomorrow I may be rescued
From all my sinking past,
And give praise all unto my lord
And may that ever last,

If you sense my hopelessness
In words that I have said,
Or felt the sorrow and the dread
In this that you have read,

I ask you pray another prayer
To God who reaches down,
And ask that he will help you too
And take you for his crown,

Yesterday I looked around
To see where I have come,
Today I think I might be found
Your prayers have overcome,

Tomorrow is a newer day
The sun is rising east,
Great praises I will have to say
"I'm going to God's feast!"

Wondrous is life that we may live
Each moment gently passing,
Our hearts, minds, lips, and ears
Take in all that's lasting,

Each day we have we choose to live
And give this day our all,
This slot continues as such until
We hear from God – The Call.

The Call

All we are and all we'll be
Is with us as we're born,
Until the day we hear a call
Upon which all is torn,

The call we hear leads us on
To another place,
A place which holds all answers
Where God is face to face,

The life we lived on this earth
Was smoke – a vapor of,
Compared to what we now will live
Abiding in God's love,

The call is not life ending
But real life there begins,
A life in which there is no end
And all around us friends,

To those behind a sadness
But to those whom called Great Joy,
To be with God the father
And of his will employed,

When e'er we hear this call so grand
No other sounds will do,
This call is at the Master's hand
When time on earth is through,

Yet called we are and all will be
When God has said, "Well done"
"I know you child and always did
I know you through my Son"

When e'er were called we open to
The life that God had planned,
For us to love, to see and view
Not made for mortal man,

These words may not seem helpful
Yet every stanza true,
And all we've been and all we are
Lives on - - when this life's through.

Celebration

With every party there's a pleasure
With every pleasure there's a dream,
With every dream there's a reason
With every reason there's a theme,

In all of our life as we know it
We must never fail to dream,
If this circle's ever broken
We unravel at the seams,

Be full of life and full of laughter
Enjoy every moment long,
In the now and the hereafter
Keep in your heart a joyful song.

The Century Past

Just a hundred years ago
God blessed us with your grace,
A tiny babe new to life
What gift to us he gave,

Years went by and time rolled on
Your life, it took a course,
Through childhood, hardship, marriage
Your solidity enforce,

Through pains, sorrows, anguish, laughs
Smiles beyond compare,
You stood your ground to let us know
You were always there,

Through the years you held us high
Your love of greatness depth,
In you we found a treasure by
The truths that your heart kept,

Today we look at century past
Of all that you have been,
And know for sure that God had cast
A strength against all men,

Your time on earth keeps us still
In traits that you have passed,
With that in mind we carry on
Until the everlast.

In Memory of
Emma C. Holmes
August 21, 1916 to January 17, 2017

The Change

Solemn are the moments
In which I view my past,
My failures and achievements
Through time aren't meant to last,

My failures I see often
They mock the things I say,
They ridicule my essence
Along life's narrow way,

The goals that I've accomplished
True as they can be,
Are only for a moment
Then time sets them free,

All that I am saying
Is that to be a man,
I must come to realize
What I must be - - I am,

If I choose to follow
A different sort of way,
I must find new meaning
In each newborn day,

Truly I can muster
Fortitude and strength,
To change what e'er I sorrow
Renewing my essence,

My hope for tomorrow
Is changing my today,
So, ridicule and sorrow
Have no place to stay,

In our most beginnings
With many toil or task,
We make our pride or sorrow
With questions that we ask,

Did we know the value
Or time the task would take?
Did we know the cost of
Our soul the toil would make?

In all our hopes and sorrows
What e'er the outcome be,
Our essence will soon follow
The outcome we have dreamed.

Debbe Nagy

If I could paint a picture
Of every place I've been,
Of all the children growing
Of memories within,

If I could paint a portrait
Of how my life has grown,
Of every crowning moment
Of moments that have flown,

If I could paint a Rembrandt
Of all that I aspire,
Of dreams not yet awakened
Of goals I hold yet higher,

The colors would speak loudly
The hues would blend and fold,
The canvas stretch out proudly
The highlights would be gold,

I'd paint my life so boldly
So, all would know and see,
This masterpiece of painting
Is what I'm meant to be.

Desire

The only person I should need
Is the one my soul would feed,
On the words that she would say
And the feelings come my way,

If I should find a soul so grand
I feel that I should take a stand,
And make this soul my very own
As we both have aged and grown,

Into a life that we choose
Not as just mere small muse,
A life worth living in our time
Trusting both our hearts and mind,

Should I ever meet this fate
I'd keep my faith and not be late,
To meet the goal of my desire
And let the faith of soul transpire,

Perchance I meet a soul of choice
That makes me glad in every voice,
I'd keep that soul within my heart
And from it wish to never part.

The Day

Yearly it comes
It sneakily strides,
It finds us each time
We've no place to hide,

Yet always it changes
It's never the same,
Yet always it knows
Our age and our name,

It never eludes us
It never will shun,
It often will rule us
From it we can't run,

It brings us excitement
With presents and glee,
Its merits entice us
Of what it will be,

It gives way to dreaming
Of what the day holds,
And when it is with us
We're another year old.

Free

The life I knew while with you
Was short and ever sweet,
My heart within it splintered
With its pulse and its beats,

At times I was so weary
My glass was ere yet filled,
My spirit weak and flimsy
Yet faith was fast instilled,

In times of sorrowed sadness
I know I touched you all,
And in total gladness
I would but to you call,

No more the tears of sorrow
So wept upon a bed,
No more waiting for tomorrow
To see what doctors said,

No more the painful restless
That kept me up all night,
No more my moans of no rest
Which gave you such a fright,

But now the splendid feeling
No pain nor sorrow known,
The rest is yet now endless
I view and see the throne,

I cheer for your tomorrow
I wait to meet you all,
I would you knew this feeling
I would you hear the call,

But not of sorrow leaving
The life you know as yours,
But that in Christ believing
In all of your life's tours,

So suddenly it happened
I could not say good-bye,
Instead, up to my times end
I reached unto the sky,

If I had those tomorrows
To life yet once again,
I'd still tell of this savior
To family and friend,

The happiness I feel here
Trumps the life I lived,
What joy is it to be where
Life to us he gives,

All I'm really saying
Is please don't weep for me,
I'm here with Christ our savior
For now -- eternally.

In Memory of
Yvette Michelle Preston
February 1, 1960 to May 13, 2015

George

The clitter and the clatter
Of every message sent,
The volume of the meaning
The tone that seems well bent,

The urgency of moment
Of those with little time,
The passing of the credit
Or guilt that seems sublime,

Each morning I will ponder
What may lie ahead,
Each evening I wander
From what I've seen and read,

The value of my presence
Seems to be the glue,
That holds the place together
Because of what I do,

Now if you ever ask me
Of why I feel this way,
The only way to answer
"Just work with me - - one day."

Graphic

To wit, to pen, to notepad
To ever flowing dreams,
To writing tablets, laptops
To graphic design schemes,

To every bit and every byte
To pixels on the page,
To fascinating colors
To themes which do not age,

Within our hearts to our mind's eye
We make our dreams come true,
With futuristic writing tools
We color them with hues,

With our minds we see it
With our tools we draw,
With our eyes we view it
The rest is oohs and awes.

I Gave

Years of roaming on the earth
From sun to newborn sun,
Always looking from my birth
New battles to be won,

My heart's fulfillment of desire
Is for my family,
To see that moment e'er transpire
I work to make it be,

I give my all, my toil of hands
The hours within my day,
I give of times of friendship
I give of my earned pay,

I give to keep the freedoms
I give to make the ends,
I give for joy and laughter
I give as heaven sends,

In this time of sorrow
As I am put to grave,
I seek no tears to borrow
For of myself - - I gave,

I gave within my living
I gave within my means,
I gave to other's giving
I gave of life and dreams.

In Memory of
Arthur W. Flournoy
Aug 1, 1934 to Sep 16, 2016

In Moments of My Mind

With tender moments flashing
In thoughts within my head,
I know that I am living
And not among the dead,

I feel my spirit calling
To times that are ahead,
I feel my soul e'er drifting
To words that God has said,

The moments that I ponder
Do keep me fresh and new,
They do not let me wander
From that which I should do,

These moments ever passing
From day to given day,
Are precious in their meanings
As they guide me on my way,

If you ever ask me
Of what I do with time,
I seek of time's true meaning
In moments of my mind.

Joey

A time it was a time on earth
I walked among God's men,
I married with a family
I had close nit friends,

I gave my all and answered call
To that my God did give,
And used my voice to entertain
Inspiring those that live,

But time has come to be called home
And there I shall now go,
To lend my voice to Angel's choir
As time of life says so,

Now I join the Angel's choir
I sing of God's great plan,
I see his glory all around
His plan for mortal man,

I sing in heaven's jubilee
The echoes of all time,
My heart's desire and spirit's wish
Is that you keep this in mind,

That heavens' not a mystery
Nor is God a myth,
That life on earth is history
And birth is God's own gift,

That time was meant for us to be
Connected soul to soul,
Now that I'm gone you will see
That life takes a new goal,

So don't be sad and miss me so
I'm still at your side,
To every prayer to God I know
We're in the by and by,

Your hearts cry and hopeful plea
Is heard by God above,
I'll see you in eternity
As I see you now my love,

I end this note to you and say
I am not far away,
Just know for sure I hear your voice
When you kneel down and pray.

The Journey Home

Under life's submission
We all hold so dear,
Not knowing of the glory
Its path we all do fear,

Those that make the journey
Have ceased from feeling fate,
Instead, they find the master
Of all who move and wait,

Life is more than seeing
And never really ends,
But transcends to plains higher
As new life there begins,

Our moments still yet precious
To all our friends and kin,
Our hearts with them e'er meshing
That life on earth we win,

Yet moments ever fleeting
As vapors passing by,
But once we've made the journey
We nevermore will die.

Life of Wonders - Thru Eyes of Son Ae Filchak

Wonders, wonders to and frow
From dawn to twilights end,
Of all the wonders I have seen
The best is of my friends,

This life is splendid certainly
In all its twists and turns,
It keeps me ever happily
As I live, I seek, I learn,

Every night and every day
Is so unique to me,
That I find a new thing to pray
Each moment that I be,

This life to me is splendid
Enriching as I grow,
My love for it is blended
With friends and family tow,

Each day I feel is gifted
A present rich and free,
My love for it is lifted
In its essence - - I am free.

Macey Grace Pruitt

My little darling
Already in school,
Can you imagine?
Enjoyment so cool,

Yesterday's playtime
Gone far away,
Readily learning
All through the day,

Can you feel excitement?
Encircling you there?
Playing with friends
Ready to share,

Usually children
In such a place,
Teach the adults
To see heaven's grace.

Mia Snow

Sleeping, sleeping peacefully
Freshly being born,
All smiles look on joyfully
From the day that's worn,

Fresh as spring and pure as snow
What joys do lie ahead?
As sleepy eyes rest from birth
What thoughts lie in her head?

None will know the mystery
Of what a baby thinks,
Yet all do know the majesty
Of joy a baby brings,

Baby Mia rest for now
Life is not to rush,
Rest, sleep then somehow
You'll one-day comfort us.

Mom

"Home is where the heart is"
Is a phrase that we all know,
Of this phrase your part is
Our hearts of whom you hold,

Many things to many folks
You have always been,
A mother and a grandmother
A wife, a sister, friend,

Often when we call your name
Depending who it's from,
Is different from each avenue
But always filled with love,

Mother, moma, grandma
These words you hear each day,
Mom, mamaw, Stella
These words all come your way,

Knowing that we love you
As much you hear us say,
Always thinking of you
And oh, so much more today.

Moms

Moms are forever in our eyes
In our hearts, our minds
They never die

They transcend unto a different place
Where forever they
Can see our face

We hold them dearly ever close
In their voice we find
Comfort most

Of gentle hands and softest heart
They are always there
From time we start

They help us grow end ever learn
We never have
Their love to earn

No sacrifice is too great to bear
They'll find a way
They'll always care

If breath of life leaves their frame
Nothing has changed
They love the same

Their spirit bids our heart to know
They're still around
To love us so

Mother's Day Wish

A mother's crowning moment
Is when she sees her child,
To take it into comfort
And hold it tender mild,

No other time is nearing
That heartfelt tender bliss,
As throughout life she's caring
For this small blessedness,

Years have come and gone again
And each year I have a wish,
A wish so true and powerful
And yet it feels selfish,

But not the case is it at all
The wish is not for me,
But wishes granted most of all
Are for friends and family,

As wishes go they are a hope
And mine is set for you,
In that you have a great Mother's Day
This day and all year through.

Mother's Watch

While with you I was watching
To let you know I care,
To let you know I love you
To teach you all to share,

To me it was great meaning
To help you see your way,
And times to give you answers
That helped you through the day,

But now that I am missing
From this life you live,
I ask once that you hear this
And to each other give,

Give of your emotions
Give of your deep love,
Give of your surroundings
I see you from above,

Just know that I am with you
I know your heartfelt tears,
I am more alive than ever
Through everlasting years,

You should feel no sorrow
Though from this life I've passed,
I am now with Jesus
And that will always last.

In Memory of my Mother
Stella B Hicks-Allen
February 25, 1942 to April 15, 2016

Moriah Cornelle Kilgore

More than oft I think of you
Of how well you may be doing,
Rarely have I heard from you
I have feelings ever looming,

Always I have thoughts of you
Had them from whence we parted,
Constantly I pray for you
On departure it all started,

Really wish I knew for sure
Not just idea in head,
Everything was good with you
Like you have seldom said,

Little times we've spoken true
Enjoying each other's voice,
Kind words have passed twixt me and you
I'd like to think it choice,

Languish has been e'er my time
Gone without knowing your state,
Oh that God keeps you healthy safe
Relying on him --I wait,

"Enjoy all that you do, know who you are, and love
life to the fullest."

My Gram

A century ago, today
The Earth became quite blessed,
The dawning of your time began
And all the Earth confessed,

"This person born of purity
With heart and comfort soul,
She'll teach, She'll reach, She'll rear and raise
With love throughout her days,

She'll hear the child of generations
As if she were her own,
She'll speak to her with utmost patience
From birth until she's grown,

She'll love each child with all her heart
She'll guide them day-by-day,
She'll hold them close in bosomed soul
She'll carefully watch them play,"

To me she's been a statute firm
She tells me of great deeds,
Her love so free and heart so pure
I feel my soul they feed,

A century ago, today
My gram to us was born,
I celebrate in every way
This page of history torn,

Ages come and ages go
But none mean more to me,
Than that of this last century
When my gram came to be.

The Loss

We oft hold on to loved ones
We keep them in our hearts,
They are so often part of us
We seek none of them parts,

From time of birth till old age
We hold to every feeling,
The voice, the look, the thoughtful ways
In our heart is always dealing,

We look to them for comfort
From all that we have seen,
When life gives to us trials
We're strong from where they've been,

We see them always standing
As mighty as oak trees,
Our secret heart's demanding
That this strength will never leave,

Never are we ready
When God calls to them home,
To lift them to high mansions
On his celestial shore to roam,

We feel the loss full mourning
Their strength we now not feel,
Not knowing that their spirit
Is just as close and real,

Holding on to all our dreams
We hold to loved ones too,
Their presence ever wielding
The strength that takes us through,

We catch a wink, a wince, a smile
We know their sad or gladness,
They lift our souls add make us soar
In times of our own sadness,

Their strength it seems won't break nor bend
Their character strong as tempered steel,
We look to them when we are wrong
To guide how we should feel,

When e'er one of these pillars high
Do leave this life and part,
We feel the mourn this life has lost
We yearn deep within our heart,

Our loss does bear no temperance
To what has come to pass,
For though we feel the loss of life
They've gone with God at last,

In all we think we've learned in life
The lesson we should know,
Is that the life we live is blind
To what makes all life flow,

We see what we believe is true
Our eyesight makes it so,
We understand and then therefore we know
How things do live and grow,

The world is all around us
Yet life is but a dream,
With all that does surround us
We know just what we've seen,

Yet life, before us started
God's spirit made that so,
If this life ends, our spirits
With him e'er do go.

In Memory of
Mary Elizabeth Young
Deceased – May 9, 2011

Niki "POOH"

Constantly I get to see
My story as it plays,
I feel a strange connection though
To my younger days,

Yesterday when I was Pooh
I'd set and read my book,
But now I live this life for real
Just simply take a look,

Christopher, the eldest
Is now my softball Jewel,
She holds my heart with every swing
And when she plays, she rules!

The ever-flouncy Tigger
Is now my bouncing Joy,
She warms my heart with movement
Much unlike my childhood toy,

When e'er I don't behold them
My story goes online,
Where I'm the narrator
In my 100 Acre time,

When e'er we leave this story
Or its fabric we will breach,
We simply move its setting
From woodland to the beach,

This story e'er continues
From day to shining day,
Now as I sit and think to ponder
I'd really have it no other way.

Our Bond

Tender are the moments
That have passed and come our way,
Remembering their splendor
In themselves in their day,

Capturing the feelings
That embraced upon our hearts,
Knowing that these feelings
Of eternal would not part,

Yesterday your presence
Held in safety of God's care,
Today he holds your spirit
And to you his heavens share,

Suddenly you see us as
No other time you could,
From the master's table
Where the Lamb of God has stood,

In the master's bidding
He has called your soul away,
But not so from our presence
As we feel you still today,

In our hearts forever
Will we feel you ever near,
In our sorrow passing
You will see it in our tears,

Holding to tomorrow
Where we'll see you once again,
In the master's presence
With your family and your friends,

There we all will gather
Just to know and sing aloud,
In that great forever
With the master of all crowds.

In Memory of
Carrie Frails
Sep 16, 1927 to Dec 20, 2016

On to...

On to future brighter goals
On to new day plans,
On to work another hold
One much better than,

On to more than I can be
On to fill a goal,
Onto futures that I see
On my seeking soul,

On to take another step
In my career's path,
Using tools my mind has kept
And will unto the last,

On to gain another ground
And plant a new foothold,
And keep in mind the friends I've found
In places new and old,

On to use my talents learned
Of what I can e'er be,
On to rewards that I've earned
Just by being me.

Phyllis

Open to all ambitions
Accepting every dream,
I always looked and listened
To those who could but dream,

Not judging nor e'er hating
Not taking a single side,
Just loving each dear moment
With you at my dear side,

Wishing we were together
Holding ourselves again,
In embrace that makes the heart pump
Reviving our love within,

Always I keep you near me
Knowing we'll always be,
Lovers from time's beginnings
Reaching eternity,

Good-bye for now my darling
I'll wait at heaven's stand,
For when we'll have tomorrow
Forever in God's plan.

In Memory of
Phyllis Ann Zoetis
Apr 7, 1962 to Sep 4, 2014

The Path of Life

Fathoms of time so deep in space
Reveal on distant shores,
That life on Earth is fleeting best
But not forever more,

We wrest this thought within our minds
To know all life's design,
But till we meet the architect
This answer we won't find,

Once we leave this body
The life of truth begins,
To know that God is closer
Than our own thoughts within,

We want for all our loved ones
To live this life we know,
Not knowing that the greater
Is where their spirits go,

These loved ones that we care for
Do see our hearts so sad,
And would love to tell us
For their soul, be glad,

No longer are they bound to
The sickness or disease,
No longer will they resound to
Deep thoughts of ill at ease,

No longer do they carry
The burdens of this life,
No longer do they tarry
Within this world of strife,

Now they're with the master
Of all of nature's plan,
Now they're with the savior
And the voice of God's command.

Rebirth

Open are our hearts and minds
That in this life true loves we find,

Each day we live and each day we give
It's moments of splendor with those whom we live,

Our passions are many our troubles are few
Our moments are lighted by faith that's anew,

Our bearings are shifted when love is unfeigned
Our life it is gifted and from it we wean,

In life's ending chapter our spirit renews
To the ever fore after in angelic pews.

In Memory of
Yvette Michelle Preston
Feb 1, 1960 to May 13, 2015

Recovery

If happiness is measured
By what we know and see,
Then all our joyous pleasures
Come from what we'll be,

At any given moment
The frame within our mind,
In any stress or sorrow
The solace we do find,

If all our joys and freedoms
Were taken far away,
Then all that still remaineth
Is thoughts within that stay,

The thoughts are of our freedoms
The joy is of our days,
The happiness within us
Is what remains and prays,

Though we may be battered
Broke and laid aside,
We'll always keep the happy
That makes our skillful stride,

With all our healing moments
In which we mend and rest,
We hold on to the knowledge
That we are at our best,

For happy is the state of mind
That knows our limit's pride,
And healing is our soul at rest
In which our health abides

Remember

Remember when you saw my face?
You felt such joy within,
Remember when you gave me place?
And helped in games to win,

Remember always caring?
Keeping me so safe?
Remember always sharing?
Feeding from your plate?

Remember always talking?
No subject kept from view?
Remember all my secrets?
Yet I never thought you knew,

You kept me in your freedom
You covered me with love,
Your words were simple comfort
As pure as snow white dove,

When e'er I lacked in motion
You gave a little tug,
If I had tears and nightmares
You fought them with a hug,

Whenever I was lonely
You held my heart, my hand,
When e'er I said, "I really can't"
You said, "Dear yes you can!"

You watched me all my years of life
A friend you were to me,
A close companion by my side
As no other mom could be,

My regret is that I see
How much you miss me now,
I wish to say that I am here
If I only can somehow,

It's you I watch, as I look ore
To see you safe from fears,
It's you I see from where I am
In a place that holds no tears,

The words I wish to tell you
From me to you today,
Is that I'll always love you
Each and every day,

Although you cannot hear me
My words remain the same,
How blessed I was to have you
Guide me through life's game,

Now I am the watcher
Tugging at your heart,
To let you know I'm with you Mom
And from that not to part.

In Memory of
Karen Ann
Deceased October 15, 2012

Reposition

Open-ended seasons
Themes to comprehend,
Issues without reason
Times to make amends,

Changing for the reason
That keeps my soul alive,
Reaching for believing
Purpose is up on high,

Daily recognizing
I am no longer me,
Instead of compromising
I choose to set me free,

Moving my position
To gain a better view,
Of all that I have ensued
And all I know I knew,

Asking for the blessing
Of all that comes my way,
To keep it ever trusted
In what I do, I say,

Given my own reasons
Of why I feel this way,
The thing that I will tell you
"It's what I choose today."

Retired

Click clack, click clack
Tic tock goes the clock,
With every passing moment
The time it never stops,

Day in day out
Always seems the same,
Meetings and agendas
And so goes the game,

Early morning dusk to dawn
Is my daily grind,
My day is filled with taskings
I have very little time,

I look for days of wishing
That these tasks be no more,
I look for days of walking
Of which I have no chore,

In that day I'll wake up
And find I have the time,
To fill my life's ambition
With each moment that is mine.

Retiring

Underneath a starry sky
I felt the night filled air,
The silent breeze and whisper trees
Seemed more than time could bear,

It seemed to be a lifetime
To finally reach this point,
In which I know tomorrow
Will be at my own choice,

Yesterday I worked so hard
At everything I did,
It kept my time and held my pace
My schedule so solid,

Today I am not grieving
To let go of the pace,
That held me as a captive
In life's e'er working race,

Tomorrow I am praying
That each day that lies ahead,
I meet with new prospective
And of the past - - to shred.

Retirement

The hours tick – the hours tock
It seems I'm always on the clock,
My time is stamped, my hours logged
My days are filled with working logs,

Each day I find much less of time
Has given way to my state of mind,
I meet the task what e'er it be
To give my all of what's in me,

All that I am and all I'll be
I seek the day I will be free,
Free from the tasks that fill my day
Free from the work that comes my way,

Free from the ties that binds my time
Free from the burdens that fill my mind,
Free from the deadlines that tax my strength
Free from the weights that are immense,

I seek the day of my desire
That sends my soul to a place higher,
I seek the day that I will rest
From the labors and the tests,

It's my desire to just retire
And do the things that I aspire,
To hone the traits of my souls hold
To make my days of young - not old,

To be the man I know I am
To hold times trust in life's grand slam,
To make my time my very own
To make my days of what I've grown,

To give my all to every moment
And make my life the purest potent,
To understand when I retire
It's time to find my each desire.

Reunion – The Lost Tie

Lost in time my parent's past
To meet and greet is here at last,
To find those near to family's hosts
To know those dear and hold them close,

Days and years have come and gone
With questions that would carry on,
The answers lie in family genes
To which were found with science means,

New living chapters lie ahead
For kin to kin to break our bread,
To know the answer of this quest
That family far is of bequest,

My journey's end is near at hand
Of which I'll join a family grand,
To e'er hold close as they are kin
And make the most of life within,

To families all both far and near
There is yet hope for wine and cheer,
To yet unite with unknown ties
Of kinship folk where our heart lies.

Sails Up

Never more at drifting
From Sun to setting Sun,
But for my children gifting
From treasures that I've won,

In this life of fortune
I've collected words and things,
Never in it sorrow
Never in it stings,

I've loved every moment
As I've sailed from sea to sea,
Wishing all my wishes
Were not all just for me,

Now the time is nearing
One setting of my Suns,
To which I say farewell
A new cruise has begun,

For me you should not worry
Of that where I have gone,
With set sails and bow pointed
I will be sailing on.

Son Ae Filchak

Somewhere in the distance
On time's eternal shore,
Near to God's existence
And close to heaven's door,

Enveloped in richness
Filled with harmony,
In ecstatic exuberance
Loves to simply be,

Clinging to the raptured
Holding to the love,
Always ever cheerful
Knowing God above.

Sounds of Life

Rushing, rushing moments forward
Never ceasing never done,
Always moving ever toward
Endless days of endless sun,

Times e'er passing never lasting
Days are numbered when we're born,
Hearts of splendor moments tender
As a vesture, feelings worn,

Life of plenty moments many
Yet the dearest moments shared,
Are of laughing moments passing
In amongst of those who cared,

In our hearts we hold truest
Those of whom we've shared our lot,
When they pass to everlasting
In us they'll never be forgot,

All our fortunes and our sorrows
Throughout life can be a snare,
If we give God our tomorrow
He will bless us with his care,

We pass from life to the hereafter
Knowing God will meet us there,
He holds our souls within his pasture
And gives to us his life to share.

In Memory of
Geraldine Joan McGowan
Jul 27, 1921 to Nov 10, 2016

Spirit Dear

I surrendered all to God today
I gave him prayer and praise,
I gave an oath to love him so
Until the end of days,

I call his name by day and night
I love to hear his name,
Lord Jesus Christ is dear to me
Into my life he came,

I wonder though how many know?
His spirit true and dear,
Perhaps they'll see him in me
If not, that's what I fear,

Today to God I knelt and prayed
I asked of Christ to hear,
To keep me close, to be his own
To keep me from that fear,

I should know God sees me
In all I say and do,
And also know he holds me
In his spirit true.

Starlight

The stars I see are shining
Gleaming bright and strong,
Their crispness and their starlight
Enduring time so long,

They twinkle and they glisten
Like actors on a stage,
They're creatures ever watching
As they view our history's page,

Their light does fall upon us
It causes more to shine,
What surfaces within us
Will meet the test of time,

The stars I now see shining
They twinkle and they glow,
They're changing with the seasons
They're part of our life's flow,

I see stars all around me
I meet them every day,
Their glisten and their twinkle
Is what they do and say.

The Road

The road I traveled lightly
Took to my easing pain,
Filled my life with laughter
And brought me home again,

Some the weary traveler
Some the heights and lows,
Some the nights and sunshine
But on that road, I'd go,

This road was rarely walked on
By any living man,
It had no blogs that talked on
Nor one to understand,

It wasn't for the weary
It wasn't for the weak,
It wasn't for the athlete
It wasn't to compete,

This road was solitary
In that it was in plan,
To find a single walker
As one of whom "I am"

On this road I carried
All struggles of my past,
At no time did I tarry
From first mile to the last,

But now the road has ended
And I ask you to see,
That with all burdens carried
This road was meant for me,

I ask you e'er so humble
To know just what I see,
A thousand roads and walkers
Here - - in eternity.

In Memory of
Joseph Henry "Joe" Riddle
March 6, 1946 to June 9, 2016

Vella Ann Newman

Vigorously waiting and looking ahead
Enduring the words that others have said,
Longing for rapture, not riches, not gold
Loving here after approaching it bold,
Allowing the reason for life and its course
Admonishing shadows of the pale horse,
Never to sorrow, never to pain
Never to welcome ill-gotten gain,
Nudging the distance from death and its part
Enjoying the sunshine and joys of the heart,
Willing to share it with all who are born
Making the best of each season worn,
Attributing to God the part in life I play
Never to be slothful - - loving life he gave.

Winds

When winds blow wild, they choose a path
Beyond our inner dreams,
They take a course of destined trails
And choose their pathful schemes,

They take directions from no man
And sway the savage beast,
They make the oceans hurl their waves
And blow both west and east,

Yet in the turmoil of their strength
And destined path they take,
Their truest journey of their time
Is in the paths they make,

In winds of season's, sorrow's past
Or winds that blow clouds clear,
The winds are destined to cross paths
And hold each other dear,

From wind to wind and breeze to breeze
All winds are from one source,
The winds unite in heaven's space
As they blow their course.

Wisdom's Cry

If wisdom is a virtue
And wisdom comes with age,
Then wise men have a calling
That comes of history's page,

As we gain in wisdom
We learn that we don't know,
The things that do elude us
Thru life and nature's flow,

In questions and in solemn
We gain an inner sight,
But virtues of the wisdom
Comes in quiet's might,

When e'er we see our future
In question of the path,
We listen to the wisdom
That guided us in past,

To all our fellow knowers
Of wisdom and its gifts,
Stay with your present pathway
As it guides you and it lifts,

Tis wise to know the future
Is molded from the past,
And wise to know that wisdom -
Is all that always lasts.

The Years

The years of blessing I have had
That keep me living on,
Of trials past and lessons learned
Of things that I am fond,

In my days of living
I've found great meaning in,
The things I've seen, I've done, I've hoped
There is a joy therein,

My years are filled with blessing
My years are filled with hope,
My years are filled with rapture
My years are filled with boasts,

My years have seen some sorrow
My years have seen some pain,
But none kept me from tomorrow
Or where I'll be again,

The portion God has measured
That make my years so grand,
To my truest knowledge
Is cause I held his hand,

If Christ be your tomorrow
His love to be your guide,
Then all your days that follow
Be golden at his side.

Years Gone By

Today a day of happiness
You celebrate with glee,
Of birthday cake and candles
With friends and family,

Yesterday has come and gone
Friends of once you've known,
Interests that you no longer have
In as much, you've grown,

All in all, a life its been
To be as you are now,
God has granted health and care
To one as such allowed,

Today's finest moment
If you listen back and look,
Is knowing how God loves you
And of your faith he took,

He calls you of his very own
You're in his heart of care,
Years of troubles sorrows past,
He'll ask you leave them there,

No longer are they yours to keep
He has purchase power,
He bought them from you years ago
In that salvation's hour,

Today's a day of happiness
But not because of age,
Your life is in God's sweet caress
His blood has paid the wage,

His spirit bids you happiness
As with you him you'll find,
He's always there and never leaves
He's been there all the time,

Now to family cake and friends
And let them all to see,
That God has blessed and kept you so
And sets your spirit free.

The Wish

On a birthday fresh and new
Is a wish for wish come true,
Not of envy, glut nor greed
Not of pious, misconceived,

Not of fabricated song
But of things that are livelong,
Things that soar the spirit high
Things that stay in by and by,

Not of glitter or fake gold
But things that always in heart hold,
A wish that keeps the wish alive
A gift that fulfills hearts contrive,

A wish that makes one's moments new
A wish that dictates things we do,
A wish that meets our heart's desire
A wish that stands time's test of fire,

A birthday wish from me to you
Is that you find God in all you do,
His gifts of his design
Lead you to eternal time,

His love from heaven's stand
His voice of his command,
Bring joy to all your heart
From which you never part.

Zion

Zion's the holy city
Of prophets it was told,
It's in the book of Samuel
King David spoke it bold,

This city never wavering
From its holy stance,
Its merits and its favors
Today's Christians e'er romance,

"We're marching to that city"
In church we hear it sung,
Yet in our hearts we're finding
We don't know where it's from,

This City and its greatness
As holy as it be,
Can now be found within us
If we'll just look and see,

Upon the seat of Zion
God rests his spirit there,
And if he is within us
Then Zion we will share,

Now if you're understanding
This message that I bring,
Then sing the songs of Zion
And let the heavens ring!